ALL  NATURE
sings

ALL NATURE
sings

An Outdoor Companion for Celebrating God's Creation

JAMES WOODROW

WESTBOW
PRESS

A DIVISION OF THOMAS NELSON

WestBow Press books may be ordered through booksellers or by contacting:

WestBow Press
A Division of Thomas Nelson
1663 Liberty Drive
Bloomington, IN 47403
www.westbowpress.com
1-(866) 928-1240

ISBN: 978-1-4497-2774-1 (sc)

Library of Congress Control Number: 2011917653

Printed in the United States of America

WestBow Press rev. date: 10/6/2011

To my parents,
who always encouraged me to go outs

ACKNOWLEDGMENTS

First, my deepest appreciation goes to my family and friends who taught me how to enjoy nature and appreciate God's wondrous creation. Included in my gratitude is Snow, my childhood friend and furry companion—always eager to join me on walks in the woods.

I also wish to thank the local Amish and Mennonite communities of southwestern Pennsylvania who quietly influenced my respect for living in harmony with the land.

Finally, the authors cited throughout this book deserve special acknowledgment for inspiring each of us with their words of praise and adoration of God's gift of creation.

CONTENTS

A WORLD OF WONDER

–1–

Introduction

"Looking at the Earth from this vantage point . . .
looking at this kind of creation and to not believe
in God, to me, is impossible."

John Glenn, Astronaut[1]

The Beauty of the Earth

"In the beginning God created . . ." is a phrase that
Christians know all too well. And we're reminded that
God is the primary mover and creator of all things by
testimonials of when 72-year old John Glenn returned to
space. Overwhelmed by God's creation as he looked down
on Planet Earth, Glenn spoke of how simply looking at
the grandeur of creation is all that's necessary to know that
there's a Creator God, a supreme being among us. Ignatius,
the Spanish knight, hermit, and Catholic priest, spoke
of "seeing God in all things,"[2] while in the Reformed
churches' confession of faith, popularly known as the *Belgic
Confession,* God's creation is described as "a most elegant
book, wherein all creatures great and small, are as so many

characters leading us to see clearly the invisible things of God."[3] God's beauty is all around us, if we're only willing to step outside and enjoy it.

Personal Reflections

Growing up in a small, farming community in Pennsylvania allowed me the benefit of enjoying a unique natural setting where the lifestyle was simple and God-centered. With the woods just a stone's throw away from our back door, I was continuously playing, hiking, biking, fishing, and enjoying the outdoors in every way possible. In our little neighborhood, we watched daffodils and tulips bloom in glorious colors each spring; climbed apple and maple trees in the summer; picked plump, juicy grapes from the arbor in the autumn; and rode sleds down our tree-lined hill in the winter. That was the beginning of my growing appreciation of God's majestic creation.

My childhood memories are endless: Sleeping under the stars on warm, summer nights, amazed at the Milky Way and countless stars, followed by the occasional shooting star . . . Exploring the hills, woods, and streams at my aunt and uncle's farm . . . Walking into the path of a skunk and running fast and furiously for safety . . . Spotting deer at night on the ridgeline along the corn fields and cow pastures. Those are just a few of my special memories of the outdoors. Think about your own experiences as a young, free spirit in God's world.

As an outdoor enthusiast now living along Southern California's coastline, God has blessed me with my own "special place" where I can commune with him daily. As I walk on the beach, I'm continuously reminded of songs of nature, such as "This is My Father's World" and "For the Beauty of the Earth," as I listen to the roaring surf, watch the graceful seagulls and pelicans in flight, and praise God for his wondrous sunsets. And as I travel this beautiful world of ours, I seek out those places known for their natural beauty and diverse wildlife, yet home is where I commune with God and his creation each day.

Why this Book?

Over the years, and with no success, I searched publishing houses for a brief, devotional book that I could carry outdoors for short, nature-inspired devotional purposes. This outdoor companion is a result of my effort to satisfy this need, one that I believe others will also find beneficial. It's a selection of classical and contemporary perspectives toward God's creation and a collection of songs, scriptures, and other inspirational words gathered to help Christians appreciate and see the natural world, God's creation, through a spiritual lens. It's a book for everyone, best used by the active outdoor enthusiast and yet a valuable source for devotional reading of nature's holy and magnificent brilliance for the armchair nature lover as well. It's also a book that requires no exotic adventures on a worldwide scale, for God's wonders can be found in any neighborhood and on every corner of the map.

The goal of this outdoor companion is to help deepen our reverence for God's creation and echo Isaiah's words to us that " …the mountains and hills will burst into song before you, and all the trees of the field will clap their hands." (Isaiah 55:12) Upon reflection on the Italian Dominican priest Thomas Aquinas' words that "Any error about creation also leads to an error about God," Steven Bouma-Prediger, author and professor of religion, concludes that "If we do not properly understand our home planet, we will not properly understand the nature and character of the God we worship and claim to serve."[4]

Contents

This book contains a variety of ideas and perspectives about God's creation as well as a set of practical principles and recommendations for communing with God as a Christian and naturalist. The first section, "A World of Wonder," consists of three parts: the first introduces the book's theme and reason for its importance, the second builds a philosophy of stewardship toward God's creation, and the third presents practices and lessons that others have learned about communing with God in nature's setting.

The next section, "Devotional Resources for Appreciating God's Creation," is also divided into three parts and builds on a collection of songs, scriptures, and quotations selected to provide you with an easy reference for your outdoor devotions. These resources are designed for reading an array of hymns, scriptures, and reflections at one sitting, contemplating only one random passage now and then, or working with a schedule of devotions. We can look at these selections as "a web of relationships, of bonding, of connectedness . . . best encapsulated not in precise definition, but in poetry and hymns, in singing and in story, the way of the Psalms," observes Mennonite author Robert Kreider.[5]

Finally, the sole focus of the third section, "Developing a Personal Approach with God," is to provide you with the practical tools for developing a closer relationship with God and nature.

Invitation

This book offers a first-step reading companion to help fellow Christians more fully appreciate God's creation. And believing that appreciation will lead us to a greater sense of stewardship, we will become actively engaged in praising God for his creation while doing our best to help God in sustaining this fragile and precious earth of ours. Use this book by yourself as your outdoor daily bread or with others when enjoying fellowship with one another around the campfire, at the picnic table, at the end of a trail, and in any way it can inspire a sense of celebration of God's wondrous creation. It provides a multitude of devotional resources and should be used freely as an outdoor companion for celebrating God's creation. Come outside, worship God in his garden, and be at one with him and his creation.

–2–

A Philosophy of Stewardship

"We have forgotten that the Apostles' Creed begins
with an affirmation of God as maker of heaven
and earth. We have forgotten that Genesis begins
with creation, not redemption, and that Revelation
ends with a redeemed, renewed creation. We have
forgotten that, in the words of St. Paul, all things
were created and hang together in Christ. While
reading the book of Scripture, we have forgotten
to read the book of nature."

Steven Bouma-Prediger, *For the Beauty of the Earth*[6]

Growing Concern for the Health of God's Creation

The 21st century is increasingly becoming known as
the "Green Century," and with good reason. Christians
everywhere are growing concerned about how we view
God's creation. Today, we're beginning to see his creation
through a different lens than in the past. Not long ago,
we interpreted Genesis 1: 26-28 (fill the earth and subdue

it, rule over every living creature) as God's message to us of "domination." Year by year, we're developing a new interpretation and appreciation for that message, one that with God's designation of humanity at the "top of the food chain" comes something we've overlooked until recently, which some call our responsibility to care for the earth.

James Watt, the first Reagan era Secretary of the Interior, is a good example of our past attitude toward God's creation. During a discussion in the early 1980s with a committee of the House of Representatives as to why his agency was acting contrary to its expressed mandate, Watt, a dedicated Christian, responded: "I do not know how many future generations we can count on before the Lord returns."[7] And many of us have believed that since Jesus is coming back soon, and since everything will be destroyed upon his return, there's no particular reason to care about the earth.

Yet, Christians are beginning to question our past rationale about how to treat the earth. After all, God spent six days creating our home and only one to create us. Clearly, he invested considerable attention to this beautiful and wondrous world that we now occupy. In many ways, the Genesis story describes God as homemaker and earth as our home. But we share this home with many other God-created inhabitants.

In the first chapter of the book of beginnings, namely, Genesis, we learn who we are, who our creator is, and of God's pleasure with his creation. The early chapters of Genesis inspire us toward a greater appreciation of reverence for creation and its creator. We find other scriptures throughout the Bible, particularly in the Old Testament, that endorse the majesty of God's creation. And many Christians over the years, such as Mennonite author Walter Klaassen, have echoed the powerful position of the 1766 Ris Confession, the Mennonite's confession of faith, which reads, "The fullness of God's Kingdom encompasses all of creation: Whenever we see a stone, tree, animal or person we see the speech of God."[8]

Our God-given Responsibility

By seeing God as creator of our precious and beautiful earth and all that it contains, we can also see him as its gardener. And it's our responsibility as caretakers of his garden to help this fragile world of ours to move in-and-out of its seasons and cycles. Thinking increasingly of ourselves as stewards of God's garden, Christians have the unique responsibility as entrusted caretakers to watch over and care for this special place we call home.

Founded in 1942, the National Association of Evangelicals advocates that Christians are to act as "faithful steward[s] of the natural world."[9] And Margaret Thatcher, former prime minister of the United Kingdom, declared: "We need our reason to teach us today that we are not . . . the lords of all we survey . . . we are the Lord's creatures, the trustees of this planet, charged today with preserving life itself . . ."[10] What powerful and inspirational declarations of this new role we find ourselves challenged to embrace.

As we have increasingly grown to appreciate that with the responsibility of leading comes serving, Jesus himself lived a life of example that to rule is to serve. So to, we are called to rule, to dominion, but we are also called to serve. We are called to responsible care for others, to lead and serve as earth-keepers, of our kind as well as other creatures often less able to survive when humanity assumes too much of a superiority complex.

Pastor and author Scott Hoezee of the Christian Reformed Church reminds us of the "ecology of praise" in which creation's "choir sings a song of high and holy praise."[11] And Joseph Sittler, a Lutheran pastor and theologian concerned about ecology well before it became a popular theme, writes:

> Man is not alone in this world . . . The creation is a community of abounding life—from the invisible microbes to the highly visible elephants, the vastness of mountains, the sweep of the seas, the expanse of land. These companions of our creaturehood are not only *there:* they are there as things without which I cannot be at all! They surround, support, nourish, delight, allure, challenge, and talk back to us.[12]

Singing the doxology and other hymns, and reading Genesis and the Psalms, all bring us to the belief that we honor our creator by caring for his masterpieces. And as caretakers of the earth, we pray the Lord's Prayer that God's will be done "on earth as it is in heaven." Again and again in many of the Psalms, we are reminded that the earth is God's, not ours. Psalm 24:1 declares that "The earth is the LORD'S, and everything in it, the world, and all who live in it . . ." And as Steven Bouma-Prediger so poignantly writes:

> Contrary to popular opinion, we do not own the earth or its creatures. God is the owner of the earth, for it was God who created it and continues to sustain it . . . God is the rightful and proper owner of the earth, but God gives us the calling to be earthkeepers. We are given the joy and the responsibility to lovingly keep the garden that is the earth . . .

Continuing his advocacy of our responsibility as earthkeepers, he provides a lengthy series of legitimate reasons. Among them, the following elements are especially noteworthy to our devotional theme:

- All of God's creatures are valuable and were placed on this earth for a reason, regardless of their usefulness to us.
- Our common dependence on God suggests that we must respect our nonhuman neighbors as we should each other as humans.
- As we grow to appreciate how fragile and finite the earth and its creatures are, living within our means allows us to conserve and preserve these precious resources.
- As part of creation's grand symphony, just as mountains sustain wild goats and trees provide birds with places to build their homes, we have a duty to all of God's creation to ensure that they

are able to praise God by living out the purpose for which God created them.

- We're all in this together, meaning that we are so bound together on this earth that our ability to flourish is interdependent. In the words of John Muir [a deeply religious environmentalist], "when we try to pick out anything by itself, we find it hitched to everything else in the universe."

- Genesis 2:15, Numbers 6, and Leviticus 25 all validate that we are to care for the earth and its creatures because "God says so." In various iterations, these Old Testament passages state that God commands us to serve and protect the earth.

- In caring for the needs of others, we are called to show the kind of care that God exhibits. In other words, as God's image-bearers, given God's concern for all creatures since he loves all creatures, so should we.

- Caring for the earth should be our natural response of gratitude for God's providential care for us and his gracious provisions. In other words, "Grace begets gratitude, and gratitude care."

This last element may be the most compelling and is reason for the title of his book, *For the Beauty of the Earth*. When given a precious gift, one that French theologian and pastor John Calvin described as "this most glorious theatre," our response should be that of "gratitude to the giver and care for the gift given."[13]

So why care for the earth? Because God commands it, because we're all in this together, because God's concerns are our concerns, because we're grateful for the wondrous gift of this earth . . .

Learning from Others

My memories of growing up in Pennsylvania are rich in observations of the Amish and Mennonite lifestyle of simplicity and frugality. In the most frequently used prayer book of the Amish, *Die Ernsthafte Christenpflicht* (The Serious Christian Duty), a line toward the end of one prayer literally translates into "help us not to harm your creatures and creation but that we may be brought to eternal salvation and may abide therein."[14] The Amish and Mennonites have a long history of living as stewards of the land. In 1940, Louis Bromfield wrote in *Pleasant Valley* that they are the only farmers in America who stayed on the land they settled and continued improving it.[15] And, in fairness, virtually all farmers and others responsible for the land over the years have understood to some extent the importance of taking care of it with what today we call "sustainable practices."

Unfortunately, our transition from an agrarian to an industrial economy, known by the Amish as "jumping the fence," proved to be the impetus for becoming more of an exploiter and less of a nurturer among those who had been responsible for the land. As Amish farmer and author David Kline writes:

> When that link to the land or the earth is severed,
> life revolves around plastic, asphalt, steel on rubber,

false-security lights—human-created things—and the weather becomes something to complain about or escape from. The beauty of the changing seasons is of minor significance. Nature becomes an adversary, something to be subdued and altered to one's liking, a resource from which to profit, seldom loved for its own sake.[16]

Today's Amish and Mennonites continue to exhibit a respect and reverence for the earth and all creation while our secular, industrialized society has moved away from such a philosophy. An Amish bishop from Pennsylvania once proclaimed, "We should conduct our lives as if Jesus would return today but take care of the land as if He would not be coming for a thousand years."[17] According to author David Kline, the Amish believe that "a theology for living should be as natural as the rainbow following a summer storm." And then they could pray, "And help us to walk gently on the earth and to love and nurture your creation and handiwork."[18] The Amish philosophy of stewardship substantiates how the larger Christian stewardship ethic toward the earth should move. In the most positive light, we should begin to "interpret [dominion] as a divine charge to be good stewards and to take care and protect the Creator's creation."[19]

Ecological Literacy

The fit between humanity and our habitat is probably a greater challenge today than at any other time in our history. Environmental scholar David Orr argues that part of finding the proper fit requires that we become ecologically literate. In his words, "The ecologically literate person has the knowledge necessary to comprehend interrelatedness, and an attitude of care or stewardship," which then must be complemented by "the practical competence required to act on the basis of knowledge and feeling." In other words, "knowing, caring, and practical competence constitute the basis of ecological literacy."[20] As Steven Bouma-Prediger advocates: "Not only must we know, we must care. And not only must we care, but we must have the wherewithal to act responsibly, informed by such knowledge and passion."[21]

But how does the concept translate into practical principles of application? Professor Orr provides a handful of elements required of us if a holistic approach to ecological literacy is to be developed. In sum, he suggests the following:

- We need to understand the importance of how humanity and nature are inextricably interconnected.
- We need to appreciate the dramatic speed of which our fragile planet is being threatened.
- We need a sense of the history of what has brought us to where we are today.
- We need to develop an ethic as to our idea of what nature is and how we agree to care for it.
- We need a new approach to technology, one that is appropriate to the scale and needs of humanity.

In conclusion, ecological literacy requires that we begin to appreciate that we live "in a world not of our own making" and one that "ought to engender humility and a thoughtful keeping of God's earth."[22]

A New Contract: Stewardship Philosophy

With the growing awareness that we are called to be God's caretakers of Planet Earth and all of his creation, we are beginning to appreciate that it is "our obligation and our opportunity" to define our role as 21st century "environmental stewards."[23] In *A Contract with the Earth,* the authors write:

> Without a green and productive Earth, clean air to breathe, and healthy streams, rivers, lakes, and oceans, life as we know it cannot survive. But where is America's environmental playbook? [We offer] a new approach to the challenges of the twenty-first century, encouraging our citizens to accept the responsibility of global environmental leadership . . . We offer this preamble . . . as a platform to frame our commitment to renew the living earth.[24]

Young people are especially beginning to embrace efforts to renew the earth. It must become a collective effort across all generations, though, appreciating that this contract must be long-term, thinking of our journey as less of a sprint and more of a marathon. Written by Mennonite children to the tune of *Jesus Loves Me,* these words are a clear example of a new environmental ethic among young people:

> Let's take care of God's good earth,
> water, forests, air, and soil.
> Don't toss out that used tinfoil.
> Ride your bike and don't burn oil.
> Love one another,
> share with each other,
> save this great earth of ours,
> and learn to do with less . . .
> Take care where you spend your cash.
> Wear used clothing, mend your rips.[25]

Returning to what can be learned from others as we build our own contract as earth's caretakers, the Amish and Mennonites believe that "living simply and sharing the world's resources" are at the heart of a kingdom lifestyle, Christian discipleship as taught in the Bible.[26] In particular, Amish "value the simple things—religion, family, land and animals. Where the world cries, 'More, more!' the Amish give thanks for 'enough' . . . the Amish believe their way of life represents a viable alternative to the modern way."[27] All Christians, all of humanity, must come to accept how connected we are to the earth.

Though many Christians may not choose to live an Amish lifestyle, avoiding modern equipment and relying on each other as a closely-knit community, we can still embrace the concept of nonconformity. Thus, a new contract with our creator and his creation requires a new philosophy of stewardship and how we see and treat the earth. We can begin with a few practical suggestions:

- Begin by changing ourselves, living faithfully as stewards, protectors, and reconcilers of God's created earth, consuming less and living lives of simplicity.
- Inform and educate others about the mission of serving as stewards of God's creation.
- Work with the poor in their efforts to protect the environment while also feeding them.
- Support and plan programs that assure protection or restoration of God's creation.
- Ultimately leave this world a better place than when we arrived.[28]

Embracing these recommendations will bring us one step closer to the practice of environmental stewardship.

Conclusion

There's little doubt that upcoming years will result in new ideas and new information as to how we build a long-term commitment of creation stewardship. Our living earth depends on our innovation and dedication to its sustainability, and it must not be all talk. As Steven Bouma-Prediger so eloquently writes:

> For the beauty of the earth. The challenge ahead is to persuade Christians that care for the earth is an integral feature of authentic Christian discipleship. It is not the gospel in its entirety, but the gospel is not gospel without it. Jesus saves, to be sure. But from what and for what does he save us? Jesus is

Lord, yes. But over whom and over what? Jesus is coming again, most certainly. But for what kind of future should we hope? To answer such fundamental questions, we need to get our theology and our ethic right. May we each be so moved by love and gratitude that we bear witness to the great good news of the gospel. In so doing we will with our lives proclaim the hope that lies within us—the hope of God's great, good future.[29]

He concludes his own Christian vision for creation care with the following, powerful words:

Perhaps at the end of the day we should heed that most passionate medieval evangelical St. Francis of Assisi, who admonished all who follow Christ to preach the gospel always, and if necessary, to use words ... Perhaps we should, like Francis, speak only when necessary and spend more time preaching our actions. That is, after all, the most genuine evangelism. The world is watching, and what we do and fail to do with respect to the earth speaks volumes.[30]

May we embrace a new contract with God's creation that includes scripture, hymns, and other insights toward a new beginning, and a new appreciation and vision for praising and serving God by caring for his creation.

–3–

Practices for Communing with God

Love all God's creation, the whole and every
grain of sand in it. Love every leaf, every ray of
God's light. Love the animals, love the plants,
love everything. If you love everything, you will
perceive the divine mystery in things. Once you
perceive it, you will begin to comprehend
it better every day.

Fyodor Dostoevsky, *The Brothers Karamazov*[31]

Why Commune Outdoors with God?

We find our God-given senses fully engaged in their ability
to see, smell, hear, touch, and taste the wonders and majesty
of our natural world. The three-dimensional elements of
nature open our senses to the opportunities and experiences
that only God's creation provides. Our very essence in
so many ways calls us to enjoy God's creation. Professor
and theologian Margaret Miles believes that "Nothing

prevents us from experiencing this universally miraculous character of the creation, except our failure to order our affections rightly and to use our senses."[32] And Russia's famed author, Dostoevsky, and many other naturalists feel a special closeness to God when they are outdoors and enveloped in God's creation. For many, nature is a special place, even a sacred place. It is a place for meditation and praise and prayer. In essence, it's our daily bread.

When our hearts are open to new experiences beyond enjoying and praising God for the beauty of the natural world, we can benefit by thinking of ourselves as students of nature and what it can teach us. As Bernard of Clairvaux, the French abbot and disciple of Francis of Assisi, wrote: "You will find more laboring in the woods than you ever will among books. Woods and stones will teach you what you can never hear from any master."[33] And in the Old Testament, we find validation of contemporary writers when we open the scriptures to Isaiah 55:12, where the prophet proclaims " . . . the mountains and the hills will burst into song, and all the trees of the field will clap their hands." If we are only willing to listen, God's handiwork is everywhere and able to speak to us and teach us.

Our appreciation for God's complex world can be enhanced with our observation of a bird building its nest or feeding its young, or the simple seeds that produce a vegetable or a flower garden, or an ant carrying a leaf of much greater weight than its own, or the tadpole as it gradually matures into a frog. We can recall the story told by Martin Buber, the famous Austrian-Jewish philosopher, of the rabbi's daily walk to a pond each morning to learn "the song with which the frogs praise God."[34] All of these wonders of creation, and so many more, are special in God's eyes, just as they should be praiseworthy to us.

In *Sacred Pathways,* Gary Thomas reminds us how sermons and books can become so routine that we must sometimes take a break from them and go outside to "the school that never closes . . . . And, see God more clearly, as well as renew yourself for your return to the fellowship with your brothers and sisters in Christ . . ."[35]

And in *Celebration of Discipline,* theologian and author in the Quaker tradition, Richard Foster, writes: "The easiest place to begin [to observe reality's events and actions] is with nature. It is not difficult to see that the created order has something to teach us."[36] If we are only willing to pay attention, we can learn from virtually everything that surrounds us in the outdoors, even the complexity and symmetry of a sunflower or a starfish.

Is it possible to talk to the animals, as did the famed English veterinarian, Dr. Doolittle, or speak to the birds, as did Francis of Assisi? Maybe we can answer this question with our observations of conversations with our own pets, whether dogs or cats. Although most of us would conclude that there is some form of basic communication and connection that occurs, we can also find contentment by just listening to birds as they sing to each other. Or could it be that they're actually singing to us? Possibly we can agree that some mysteries of God simply aren't meant to be understood, but rather just enjoyed and appreciated for the pleasure they create.

The outdoors also can help us to reshape our priorities, which are often different than God's. Only God knows what we need to hear, and when we are in the midst of his creation and if we are willing to let go of our worries and other human distractions, allowing God to be the initiator of our spiritual walk, the experience can reshape our agenda. And in times of decision or despair as well as joy and thankfulness, God's cathedral (or chapel) is where we can go to grow "nearer to God," in the words of the song writer. Or, to put things into perspective, as we "consider the birds of the air or the lilies of the field," in the words of Jesus, we must trust that God is taking care of us during uncertain times.

Thankfully, there is no escaping God. He is both invisible and everywhere. But to fully appreciate him, we must fight the indoor society that we've become, regularly venturing back into the outdoors. The outdoors, in contrast to the religious edifices built by human hands, is a place where many of us can connect with God in special ways. Any place in the out-of-doors can be God's cathedral. And sometimes, we can even find a special connectedness between nature and God's word, such as when we walk through a vineyard or under a grape arbor and appreciate Christ's message that he is the vine and we are the branches.[37]

The outdoors can also provide us with an incredible source of healing power and many Christians over the years have gone into the wilderness, the desert, the oceans, and skies, to find God during difficult times. With the creation fully engaging our senses as well as every particle of our cognitive and emotional being, many of us find that we can meditate and pray outdoors better than anywhere else. Susan Power Bratton, Christian naturalist and author, proclaims:

> Experiencing the beauty and peace of God in nature is not a substitute for direct interaction with the regenerative powers of the Creator, but …the mending and binding so necessary to heal our stress filled lives may flow through creation. For the spiritually oppressed or the socially injured, a pleasing or quiet natural environment can help provide spiritual release. Resting by a clear, free-running river or sitting on a sunny slope in blooming desert grassland can bring peace and joy into very clouded souls.[38]

And Gary Thomas, bestselling author and writer-in-residence at a Baptist congregation, learned over the years that he'll always be a rich man in the outdoors "regardless of personal pain, vocational frustration or success, financial excess or lack."[39] We each must learn to value nature's healing power over our stress-filled lives.

Learning from Others

What can we learn from others as we strive to understand nature's role in our spiritual walk? Role models are abundant, but even the ultimate master teacher, Jesus himself, needed to find quiet, for that matter, lonely places where he could rest, pray, and recharge his batteries. Jesus even taught his disciples to seek quiet places, departing by boat to find some peace and quiet (Mark 6:30-32). We also need time by ourselves, as well as with others, in nature, giving us the chance to reflect on our place in God's creation. In *Sacred Pathways,* we find that three elements are necessary for us to "create a space of time, quiet, and isolation before we can truly see God."[40] They are:

First, believe. As Martin Luther insisted: "Now if I believe in God's Son and bear in mind that He became man, all creatures will appear a hundred times more beautiful to me than before. Then I will properly appreciate the sun, the moon, the stars, trees, apples, pears, as I reflect that he is Lord over and the center of all things."[41] And in Gary Thomas' words: "If we don't appreciate the outdoors, then maybe we don't appreciate the Creator . . . So the first way to become awakened is to seek the Creator behind the creation. Luther called creation the 'mask of God.' A mask partially conceals, but it also tells us that something is behind the mask."[42]

Second, perceive. Bonaventure, one of Francis of Assisi's disciples, instructs us on how we might seek God in the outdoors:

> . . . consider the greatness of creation—mountains, sky, and oceans—that clearly portrays the immensity of the power, wisdom, and goodness of the triune God. Next, look at the multitude of creation—a forest has more plant and animal life than you could examine in a lifetime and shows us how God is capable of doing many things at once. Those who wonder how God can hear so many prayers uttered simultaneously have been out of the forest too long.

Finally, examine the beauty of creation—see the beauty of rocks and their shapes, the beauty of colors and shades, the beauty of individual elements (like trees), and the beauty of overall composition (like forests). God's beauty cannot be revealed through one form, but is so vast and infinite it can fill an entire world with wonder. The outdoors also speaks of God's abundance. We've talked much about the forest, but stand barefoot in a desert or on a beach and try to guess how many grains of sand are under your feet, or within your sight, or on all the beaches and deserts of the world. We serve a God of plenty, whose mercy and love are inexhaustible.[43]

As Gary Thomas so aptly writes, "For the true Christian naturalist, creation is nothing less than a sanctuary, a holy place that invites you to prayer."[44]

Third, receive. We all live in unique places, whether near the ocean, lakes, woods, meadows, or mountains. Some are more wondrous than others yet all are God's creation. Make the most of wherever you live. Appreciate, receive, and enjoy nature's wonders. Sometimes, all that's necessary is a walk across the field, along the beach, around the lake, or on the forest trail. As he describes of his own walks, "There God planted new directions in my heart, and I lingered at that bridge, enjoying a rich time of worship . . . I left the woods deeply in love with a God who shares his heart and purposes with me."[45]

May we each learn to believe, perceive, and receive God's wondrous blessings of nature.

Best Practices

There is immense value to learning from others who have been practicing their craft for so many years that it becomes an art form. We can also learn from others as we attempt to become more comfortable about communing with God through his creation. Indeed, there are valuable practices from which we can benefit from in God's manifest expression in a meadow or any of his glorious blessings of nature. As we explore the lessons that follow, both for individuals and groups, be prepared to listen openly and actively to God as he runs his course through you.

When we get close to the earth, we can develop a deeper appreciation for God's creation. Many of us need a special place where we can meditate and reflect. For me, in addition to my daily beach walks, one of my favorite spiritual retreats is in the Sierra Nevada mountains. There, I'm alive and reinvigorated among alpine lakes where the air's pure and clean and where I can go to my "special place" to walk across the wood-planked bridge and sit and reflect while gazing across the lake and through the tree limbs and leaves to the mountains beyond. Most of us need to find a solitary place, as did Jesus, to be with God and his creation.

The ways in which we commune may include walking, canoeing, biking, or simply sitting. And nature's blessings are more accessible than we sometimes appreciate. With so many of us now living in cities and suburbs, some of the best nature walks and trails are in city parks, among them the "Naturalist's Walk" in New York City's Central Park.[46]

One of our greatest challenges is to overcome the need to feel like we must own everything to enjoy it. God shares his creation with everyone, allowing us all to have equal rights to simply appreciate nature's gift to us. In *Celebration of Discipline,* Richard Foster elaborates on the value of appreciating nature without feeling like we must own a piece of it:

> Owning things is an obsession in our culture. If we own it, we feel we can control it; and if we can control it, we feel it will give us more pleasure. The idea is an illusion. Many things in life can be enjoyed without possessing or controlling them. Share things. Enjoy the beach without feeling you have to buy a piece of it. Enjoy public parks . . . Develop a deeper appreciation for the creation. Get close to the earth. Walk whenever you can. Listen to the birds—they are God's messengers. Enjoy the texture of grass and leaves. Marvel in the rich colors everywhere. Simplicity means to discover once again that 'the earth is the Lord's and the fullness thereof' (Psa. 24:1).[47]

In recent years, it has become clear that earth's resources are limited, and that the sun's energy seems to be the only limitless, dependable resource in the future. Hence, we return to the Amish lifestyle of "enough is enough" as we attempt to understand how we can live in a world with limited resources. In fact, the Christian viewpoint may require a new maxim, "Act so to live within your means." And although the adjustment phase may be painful, we can begin setting an example for others in the world by joyfully proclaiming, "I have what I need."[48]

Increasingly, frugality will become associated with our caretaker role of God's creation. We must learn to use sparingly God's provisions, understanding that the earth is finite, thus cultivating the "virtues of self-restraint and frugality."[49] As we have seen among the Amish and Mennonite lifestyles, the historic Shaker hymn tells of a similar priority on frugality: "Tis a gift to be simple, 'tis a gift to be free, 'tis a gift to come down where you ought to be; and when we find ourselves in the place just right, 'twill be in the valley of love and delight." When we accept a gift, we should do it joyfully, just as in the hymn's refrain, we should live a joyful life of simplicity.[50]

Although unfashionable in our materialistic culture, author and poet Henry David Thoreau reaffirms its truth, "Most of the luxuries, and many of the so called comforts of life, are not only not indispensable, but positive hindrances to the elevation of mankind."[51] And in this context, we are quickly reminded of Jesus' insistence that we can't serve both God and the obsession of wealth. As the maxim states, "Live simply so that others may simply live." As we seek ways to sustain our fragile earth, God's creation, we "live simply in order to unclutter our lives so as to focus on what is truly important."[52]

Increasingly more churches, colleges, and other Christian communities are also providing opportunities for their members to collectively as groups and fellowships connect with God through nature. For instance, in the summer months, a group of Christians meet for Sunday morning worship and fellowship at the beach nearby. And as a college professor, it's refreshing to watch my students studying, playing, and praying together during warm, sunny days. Although we've become an indoor society, the outdoors continues to call us, and our ongoing desire to get close to nature offers a wonderful opportunity for churches and others to enjoy fellowship with one another while communing in God's chapel.

Dreaming of what might be, it also may be time for more outdoor ministries, translating into more reading, talking, and reflecting on God's creation as well as how we can become more involved as a citizenry (and as congregations) as caretakers of our communities. Possibly it might take us into the woods and fields for more devotionals or encourage us to get involved in tree-planting campaigns or maybe we give thanks to God by creating outdoor ministries where we're cleaning-up beaches, parks, or roadside litter. For many years, Christians in my fellowship looked forward to participating in the Yosemite Encampment in California, where we met at the "Chapel in the Woods" for a host of events, all which could have been conducted in a church building, but we wanted to commune with God in one of the most breathtaking wonders of his creation.

It all begins with us, particularly as individuals, but also as groups and communities. And as we seek to understand the forms of communing with God in nature, we can learn much from others who have been steadfastly exploring how we might fulfill our needs to admire God's creation.

DEVOTIONAL RESOURCES FOR APPRECIATING GOD'S CREATION

-4-

Hymns and Songs
of Praise

Throughout history, there are countless examples of Christians who were moved by God's creation and penned the words to great songs of the church that continue in popularity to this day. Ill and losing his sight yet vividly recalling the beauty of all God's creatures, Francis of Assisi praised his creator by writing the words to "All Creatures of Our God and King." Folliot Pierpoint, inspired by the English countryside in late spring, penned the words to "For the Beauty of the Earth." Henry van Dyke, reflecting upon the joy of the sunshine, flowers, birds, and mountains, wrote "Joyful, Joyful We Adore Thee." And Maltbie Babcock, a pastor in New York, always began his walk in the woods by saying, "I'm going out to see my Father's world," where we find the phrase, "All nature sings."

When we acknowledge that "the earth is the Lord's," we quickly grow appreciative of this sacred gift that God shares with us. Lawrence Hart persuasively and poetically writes that "the earth is a beautiful song God made visible."[53] As a natural outpouring of our gratitude, we can joyfully sing, read aloud, or quietly meditate on the lyrics of a multitude of nature-inspired hymns and songs.

This collection of hymns and songs has been chosen from *Songs of Faith and Praise*[54] and is arranged in alphabetical order (by hymn title). Liberty was taken to edit some of the songs, particularly when verses were less oriented toward the theme of celebrating God's creation. Make a joyful sound unto the Lord!

All Creatures of Our God and King

All creatures of our God and King,
Lift up your voice and with us sing
Alleluia, Alleluia!
Thou burning sun with golden beam,
Thou silver moon with softer gleam.

Thou rushing wind that art so strong,
Ye clouds that sail in heav'n along
Alleluia, Alleluia!
Thou rising morn in praise rejoice,
Ye lights of evening, find a voice.

Francis of Assisi, 1226;
translated by William Henry Draper

James Woodrow

All Things Bright and Beautiful

The little flow'r that opens, The little bird that sings
God made their glowing colors, He made their tiny wings.

The cold wind in the winter, The pleasant summer sun,
The ripe fruits in the garden, He made them ev'ry one.

He gave us eyes to see them, And lips that we might tell
How great is God Almighty, Who has made all things well.

*All things bright and beautiful, Creatures great and small,
All things wise and wonderful, The Lord God made them
all.

C. F. Alexander, 1848
*Refrain

Can You Count the Stars?

Can you count the stars of evening
That are shining in the sky?
Can you count the clouds that daily
Over all the world go by?
God the Lord, who doth not slumber,
Keepeth all the boundless number:
But He careth more for thee,
But He careth more for thee.

Can you count the birds that warble
In the sunshine all the day?
Can you count the little fishes
That in sparkling waters play?
God the Lord, their number knoweth,
For each one His care He showeth:
Shall He not remember thee?
Shall He not remember thee?

Johann Hey, 1921; translated by Elmer L. Jorgenson

Fairest Lord Jesus

Fairest Lord Jesus!
Ruler of all nature!
O Thou of God and man the Son!
Thee will I always cherish,
Thee will I honor,
Thou, my soul's glory, joy, and crown.

Fair are the meadows,
Fairer still the woodlands,
Robed in the blooming garb of spring;
Jesus is fairer,
Jesus is purer,
Who makes the woeful heart to sing.

Fair is the sunshine,
Fairer still the moonlight,
And all the twinkling starry host:
Jesus shines brighter,
Jesus shines purer,
Than all the angels heav'n can boast.

17th Century German Hymn, 1677; translated by Richard
S. Willis

For the Beauty of the Earth

For the beauty of the earth,
For the beauty of the skies,
For the love which from our birth
Over and around us lies:

For the beauty of each hour
Of the day and of the night,
Hill and vale, and tree, and flow'r,
Sun and moon, and stars of light:

*Lord of all, to Thee we raise
This our sacrifice of praise.

Folliot S. Pierpont, 1864
*Refrain

God Moves in a Mysterious Way

God moves in a mysterious way,
His wonders to perform;
He plants His footsteps in the sea,
And rides upon the storm.

William Cowper, 1774

Give to Our God Immortal Praise

He built the earth, He spread the sky,
And fixed the starry lights on high:
Wonders of grace to God belong;
Repeat His mercies in your song.

He fills the sun with morning light;
He bids the moon direct the night:
His mercies ever shall endure,
When suns and moons shall shine no more.

Isaac Watts, 1719

God of Our Fathers

God of our fathers, whose almighty hand
Leads forth in beauty all the starry band
Of shinning worlds in splendor thru the skies
Our grateful songs before Thy throne arise.

Daniel C. Roberts, 1876

God, Who Made the Earth and Heaven

God, who made the earth and heaven, darkness and light:
You the day for work have given, for rest the night.
May Your angel guards defend us, slumber sweet Your mercy send us,
Holy dreams and hopes attend us all thru the night.

Reginald Heber, 1827

Hallelujah, Praise Jehovah

Hallelujah, praise Jehovah!
From the heavens praise His name;
Praise Jehovah in the highest;
All His angels praise proclaim,
All His hosts together praise Him,
Sun and moon and stars on high;
Praise Him, O ye heav'n of heavens,
And ye floods above the sky.

Let them praises give Jehovah!
They were made at His command;
Them forever He established:
His decree shall ever stand,

From the earth, O praise Jehovah,
All ye floods, ye dragons all,
Fire and hail and snow and vapors,
Stormy winds that hear Him call.

All ye fruitful trees and cedars,
All ye hills and mountains high,
Creeping things and beasts and cattle,
Birds that in the heavens fly,
Kings of earth and all ye people,
Princes great, earth's judges all;
Praise His name, young men and maidens,
Aged men and children small.

*Let them praises give Jehovah,
For His name alone is high,
And His glory is exalted,
Far above the earth and sky.

William J. Kirkpatrick, 1893
*Refrain

Holy, Holy, Holy

Holy, holy, holy! Lord God Almighty!
All Thy works shall praise Thy name, in earth, and sky, and sea;
Holy, holy, holy! merciful and mighty!
God in three Persons, blessed Trinity.

Reginald Heber, 1826

I Sing the Mighty Power of God

I sing the mighty pow'r of God, That made the mountains rise;
That spread the flowing seas abroad, and built the lofty skies.
I sing the wisdom that ordained The sun to rule the day;
The moon shines full at His command, And all the stars obey.

I sing the goodness of the Lord, That filled the earth with food;
He formed the creatures with His word, And then pronounced them good.
Lord, how Thy wonders are displayed, Where'er I turn my eye:
If I survey the ground I tread, Or gaze upon the sky!

There's not a plant or flow'r below, But makes Thy glories known;
And clouds arise, and tempests blow, By order from Thy throne;
While all that borrows life from Thee Is ever in Thy care,
And ev'rywhere that man can be, Thou, God, are present there.

Isaac Watts, 1715

Joyful, Joyful We Adore Thee

All Thy works with joy surround Thee, Earth and heav'n reflect Thy rays,
Stars and angels sing around Thee, Center of unbroken praise;
Field and forest, vale and mountain, Flowery meadow, flashing sea,
Chanting bird and flowing fountain Call us to rejoice in Thee.

Henry van Dyke, 1907

Let Every Heart Rejoice and Sing

He bids the sun to rise and set;
In heav'n His pow'r is known;
And earth, subdued to Him, shall yet
Bow low before His throne.

*While the rocks and the **rills,
While the vales and the hills,
A glorious anthem raise;
Let each prolong the grateful song,
And the God of our fathers praise,
And the God of our fathers praise.

Henry S. Washburne, 1842
*Refrain (partial)
**Rills=brook

James Woodrow

Let the Whole Creation Cry

Let the whole creation cry: Alleluia!
"Glory to the Lord on High" Alleluia!
Heaven and earth, awake and sing, Alleluia!
God is God and therefore King, Alleluia!

Praise Him, all ye hosts above, Alleluia!
Ever bright and fair in love! Alleluia!
Sun and moon, lift up Your voice; Alleluia!
Night and star, in God rejoice, Alleluia!

Stopford A. Brooke, 1881

Praise the Lord

Praise the Lord, ye heav'ns, adore Him!
Praise Him, angels, in the height;
Sun and moon rejoice before Him;
Praise Him, all ye stars of light.

The Founding Hospital Collection, London, 1796

Praise the Lord! O Heavens

Praise the Lord! O heav'ns adore Him; Praise Him, angels in the height;

Sun and moon, bow down before Him; Praise Him, shining stars of light.

Praise the Lord, for He hath spoken; Worlds His mighty voice obeyed;

Laws which never shall be broken For their guidance He has made.

The Founding Hospital Collection, London, 1796

The Spacious Firmament on High

The spacious firmament on high, With all the blue, ethereal sky,
And spangled heav'ns, a shining frame, Their great Original proclaim:
Th' unwearied sun from day to day Does his Creator's power display,
And publishes to ev'ry land The work of an almighty hand.

Soon as the evening shades prevail, The moon takes up the wondrous tale,
And nightly to the list'ning earth Repeats the story of her birth;
While all the stars that round her burn, And all the planets in their turn,
Confirm the tidings as they roll, And spread the truth from pole to pole.

What tho in solemn silence all move round this dark terrestrial ball?
What tho no real voice nor sound Amid their radiant orbs be found?
In reason's ear they all rejoice, And utter forth a glorious voice,
Forever singing as they shine, "The hand that made us is divine."

Joseph Addison, 1812

This Is My Father's World

This is my Father's world,
And to my list'ning ears,
All nature sings, and round me rings
The music of the spheres.
This is my Father's world,
I rest me in the thought
Of rocks and trees, of skies and seas;
His hand the wonders wrought.

This is my Father's world,
The birds their carols raise;
The morning light, the lily white
Declare their Maker's praise.
This is my Father's world,
He shines in all that's fair;
In the rustling grass I hear Him pass,
He speaks to me everywhere.

Maltbie D. Babcock, 1901

Walking Alone at Eve

Walking alone at eve and viewing the skies afar,
Bidding the darkness come to welcome each silver star;
I have a great delight in the wonderful scenes above,
God in His pow'r and might is showing His truth and love.

Thomas R. Sweatmon, 1917

–5–

Holy Scriptures
Praising the Creator
(and Sustainer)

For Christians, "the Bible plays a central role in theological reflection—indeed, in all of life. We are people of the Book."[55] And few authors have described the Bible's relationship to God and nature as Wendell Berry, when he wrote:

> I don't think it is enough appreciated how much an outdoor book the Bible is. It is . . . a book open to the sky. It is best read and understood outdoors, and the farther outdoors the better. Or that has been my experience of it . . . because outdoors we are confronted everywhere with wonders; we see that the miraculous is not extraordinary but the common mode of existence. It is our daily bread.[56]

So, it's obvious that we go to the scriptures for inspiration as to how God created and continues to sustain this magnificent universe that we occupy, if only for a brief time. Comparatively, it's striking to see how much more focused the Old Testament is on God's creation than the New Testament. It's understandable, though, when we appreciate the different emphases in the two testaments.

While the Old Testament focuses on the creation story, King David's prolific songs of praise about God's creation and God's new and evolving relationship with his people, the New Testament emphasizes Jesus, the church, and our lives in Christ. The New Testament, though, is far from void of testimony to God's creation, especially of the continuing acts of God in sustaining creation. Jesus certainly made reference to his Father's creation in his lessons and parables, using illustrations of the mustard seed, living streams, birds of the air, lilies of the field, and other descriptions of nature to make his points. Even where he preached and taught was often outdoors. And where did he spend his final hours? In the quietness of the Garden of Gethsemane.

Throughout the Old and New Testaments, we learn to appreciate God's design of all creation for his pleasure as well as ours. The scriptures that follow were chosen to serve as a source of inspiration as we commune with God in nature are excerpts from *The Holy Bible, New International Version*.[57] They are organized in sequential order (by book in the Bible). Liberties were taken to title the passages for easy reference and occasionally to eliminate phrases, using ellipses, less applicable to God's creation of nature (vs. quoting complete verses).

Old Testament

Beginning at the beginning, we are reminded that God's provisions for Adam and Eve were not of brick and mortar, but of Eden, a beautiful garden where he walked with them among what we can only speculate to be a breathtakingly beautiful setting. As we turn to Old Testament passages for the wealth of testimony and confession that "God is Creator," we marvel at the joy and praise of the creation shared by prophet, king, and messenger of God's majesty.

Creation: Day 1

In the beginning God created the heavens and the earth. Now the earth was formless and empty, darkness was over the surface of the deep, and the Spirit of God was hovering over the waters. And God said, "Let there be light," and there was light. God saw that the light was good, and he separated the light from the darkness. God called the light "day," and the darkness he called "night." And there was evening, and there was morning—the first day.

Genesis 1:1-5 (The Creation Story)

Creation: Day 2

And God said, "Let there be an expanse between the waters to separate water from water." So God made the expanse and separated the water under the expanse from the water above it. And it was so. God called the expanse "sky." And there was evening, and there was morning—the second day.

Genesis 1:6-8 (The Creation Story)

Creation: Day 3

And God said, "Let the water under the sky be gathered in one place, and let dry ground appear." And it was so. God called the dry ground "land," and the gathered waters he called "seas." And God saw that it was good. Then God said, "Let the land produce vegetation: seed-bearing plants and trees on the land that bear fruit with seed in it, according to their various kinds." And it was so. The land produced vegetation: plants bearing seed according to their kinds and trees bearing fruit with seed in it according to their kinds. And God saw that it was good. And there was evening, and there was morning—the third day.

Genesis 1:9-13 (The Creation Story)

Creation: Day 4

And God said, "Let there be lights in the expanse of the sky to separate the day from the night, and let them serve as signs to mark seasons and days and years, and let them be lights in the expanse of the sky to give light on the earth." And it was so. God made two great lights—the greater light to govern the day and the lesser light to govern the night. He also made the stars. God set them in the expanse of the sky to give light on the earth, to govern the day and the night, and to separate light from darkness. And God saw that it was good. And there was evening, and there was morning—the fourth day.

Genesis 1:14-19 (The Creation Story)

Creation: Day 5

And God said, "Let the water teem with living creatures, and let birds fly above the earth across the expanse of the sky." So God created the great creatures of the sea and every living and moving thing with which the water teems, according to their kinds, and every winged bird according to its kind. And God saw that it was good. God blessed them and said, "Be fruitful and increase in number and fill the water in the seas, and let the birds increase on the earth." And there was evening, and there was morning—the fifth day.

And God said, "Let the land produce living creatures according to their kinds: livestock creatures that move along the ground, and wild animals, each according to its kind." And it was so. God made the wild animals according to their kinds, the livestock according to their kinds, and all the creatures that move along the ground according to their kinds. And God saw that it was good.★

Genesis 1:20-25 (The Creation Story)

★God continued, creating male and female on the sixth day and resting on the seventh.

God's Covenant with Noah and Creation

And God said, "This is the sign of the covenant I am making between me and you and every living creature with you, a covenant for all generations to come: I have set my rainbow in the clouds, and it will be the sign of the covenant between me and the earth. Whenever I bring clouds over the earth and the rainbow appears in the clouds, I will remember my covenant between me and you and all living creatures of every kind. Never again will the waters become a flood to destroy all life. Whenever the rainbow appears in the clouds, I will see it and remember the everlasting covenant between God and all living creatures of every kind on the earth."

Genesis 9:12-16

Created in Six Days

For in six days the LORD made the heavens and the earth, the sea, and all that is in them . . .

Exodus 20:11

The Light of Morning: David's Last Words

. . . he is like the light of morning at sunrise on a cloudless morning, like the brightness after rain that brings the grass from the earth.

2 Samuel 23:4

David's Prayer

Yours, O LORD, is the greatness and the power and the glory and the majesty and the splendor, for everything in heaven and earth is yours . . . you are the ruler of all things.

1 Chronicles 29:11-12

How Majestic Is Your Name

O LORD, our Lord, how majestic is your name in all the earth! You have set your glory above the heavens . . .

When I consider your heavens, the work of your fingers, the moon and the stars, which you have set in place, what is man that you are mindful of him, the son of man that you care for him? You have made him a little lower than the heavenly beings and crowned him with glory and honor.

You made him ruler over the works of your hands; you put everything under his feet: all flocks and herds, and the beasts of the field, the birds of the air, and the fish of the sea, all that swim the paths of the seas.

The LORD, our Lord, how majestic is your name in all the earth!

Psalm 8

The Glory of God

The heavens declare the glory of God; the skies proclaim the work of his hands. Day after day they pour forth speech; night after night they display knowledge. There is no speech or language where their voice is not heard. Their voice goes out into all the earth, their words to the ends of the world.

In the heavens he has pitched a tent for the sun, which is like a bridegroom coming forth from his pavilion, like a champion rejoicing to run his course. It rises at one end of the heavens and makes its circuit to the other; nothing is hidden from its heat.

Psalm 19:1-6

Green Pastures

The Lord is my shepherd, I shall not be in want. He makes me lie down in green pastures, he leads me beside quiet waters, he restores my soul.

Psalm 23:1-3

The LORD's Earth

The earth is the LORD's, and everything in it, the world, and all who live in it; for he founded it upon the seas and established it upon the waters.

Psalm 24:1-2

The LORD's Word

By the word of the LORD were the heavens made, their starry host by the breath of his mouth.

Psalm 33:6

His Characteristics, His Creation

Your love, O LORD, reaches to the heavens, your faithfulness to the skies. Your righteousness is like the mighty mountains, your justice like the great deep.

Psalm 36:5-6

Streams and Waterfalls

As the deer pants for streams of water, so my soul pants for you, O God . . . Deep calls to deep in the roar of your waterfalls; all your waves and breakers have swept over me. By day the LORD directs his love, at night his song is with me—a prayer to the God of my life.

Psalm 42:1, 7-8

Praise to God, Ruler of the Earth

How awesome is the LORD Most high, the great King over all the earth! For God is the King of all the earth; sing to him a psalm of praise.

Psalm 47:2, 7

The Mighty One Speaks

The Mighty One, God, the LORD, speaks and summons the earth from the rising of the sun to the place where it sets . . . for every animal of the forest is mine, and the cattle on a thousand hills. I know every bird in the mountains, and the creatures of the field are mine.

Psalm 50:1, 10-11

Creator and Sustainer

You answer us with awesome deeds of righteousness, O God our Savior, the hope of all the ends of the earth and of the farthest seas, who formed the mountains by your power, having armed yourself with strength, who stilled the roaring of the seas, the roaring of their waves, and the turmoil of the nations. Those living far away fear your wonders; where morning dawns and evening fades you call forth songs of joy.

You care for the land and water it; you enrich it abundantly. The streams of God are filled with water to provide the people with grain, for so you have ordained it. You drench its furrows and level its ridges; you soften it with showers and bless its crops. You crown the year with your bounty, and your carts overflow with abundance. The grasslands of the desert overflow; the hills are clothed with gladness. The meadows are covered with flocks and the valleys are mantled with grain; they shout for joy and sing.

Psalm 65:5–13

It Was You

It was you who split open the sea by your power . . . It was you who opened up springs and streams; you dried up the ever flowing rivers. The day is yours, and yours also the night; you established the sun and moon. It was you who set all the boundaries of the earth; you made both summer and winter.

Psalm 74:13, 15-17

The Sparrow and Swallow

Even the sparrow has found a home, and the swallow a nest for herself, where she may have her young—a place near your altar, O LORD Almighty, my King and my God.

Psalm 84:3

North and South

The heavens are yours, and yours also the earth; you founded the world and all that is in it. You created the north and the south . . .

Psalm 89:11–12

The LORD of All the Earth

The LORD reigns, let the earth be glad; let the distant shores rejoice . . . His lightning lights up the world . . . The heavens proclaim his righteousness, and all the peoples see his glory.

Psalm 97:1, 4, 6

The Earth's Foundations

In the beginning you laid the foundations of the earth, and the heavens are the work of your hands.

Psalm 102:25

Many Are Your Works, O LORD!

O LORD my God, you are very great . . .

He makes springs pour water into the ravines; it flows between the mountains. They give water to all the beasts of the field; the wild donkeys quench their thirst. The birds of the air nest by the waters; they sing among the branches. He waters the mountains from his upper chambers; the earth is satisfied by the fruit of his work. He makes grass grow for the cattle . . . The trees of the LORD are well watered, the cedars of Lebanon that he planted. There the birds make their nests; the stork has its home in the pine trees. The high mountains belong to the wild goats; the crags are a refuge for the *coneys.

The moon marks off the seasons, and the sun knows when to go down. You bring darkness, it becomes night, and all the beasts of the forest prowl. The lions roar for their prey and seek their food from God. The sun rises, and they steal away; they return and lie down in their dens . . . How many are your works, O LORD! In wisdom you made them all; the earth is full of your creatures. There is the sea, vast and spacious, teeming with creatures beyond number—living things both large and small . . .

I will sing to the LORD all my life; I will sing praise to my God as long as I live. May my meditation be pleasing to him, as I rejoice in the LORD . . . Praise the LORD, O my soul. Praise the LORD.

Psalm 104:1, 10-14, 16-22, 24-25, 33-35

*The hyrax or rock badger

Blessings of the Creator

May you be blessed by the LORD, the Maker of heaven and earth.

Psalm 115:15

Praise to God in Creation

I know that the LORD is great, that our Lord is greater than all gods. The LORD does whatever pleases him, in the heavens and on the earth, in the seas and all their depths. He makes clouds rise from the ends of the earth; he sends lightning with the rain and brings out the wind from his storehouses.

Psalm 135:5-7

His Love Endures Forever

Give thanks to the LORD, for he is good . . . to him who alone does great wonders, who by his understanding made the heavens, who spread out the earth upon the waters, who made the great lights—the sun to govern the day, the moon and stars to govern the night . . . Give thanks to the God of heaven.

Psalm 136:1, 4-9, 26

Praise to the LORD from Creation

Praise the LORD . . . Praise him, sun and moon, praise him, all you shining stars. Praise him, you highest heavens and you waters above the skies. Let them praise the name of the LORD, for he commanded and they were created. He set them in place for ever and ever; he gave a decree that will never pass away.

Praise the LORD from the earth, you great sea creatures and all ocean depths, lightning and hail, snow and clouds, stormy winds that do his bidding, you mountains and all hills, fruit trees and all cedars, wild animals and all cattle, small creatures and flying birds . . .

Let them praise the name of the LORD, for his name alone is exalted; his splendor is above the earth and the heavens.

Psalm 148:1, 3-10, 13

His Wisdom, Understanding, and Knowledge

By wisdom the LORD laid the earth's foundations, by understanding he set the heavens in place; by his knowledge the deeps were divided, and the clouds let drop the dew.

Proverbs 3:19–20

The Work of God

If clouds are full of water, they pour rain upon the earth. Whether a tree falls to the south or to the north, in the place where it falls, there will it lie. Whoever watches the wind will not plant; whoever looks at the clouds will not reap.

As you do not know the path of the wind . . . so you cannot understand the work of God, the Maker of all things.

Ecclesiastes 11:3-5

The Lord God Almighty Is His Name

He who forms the mountains, creates the wind, and reveals his thoughts to man, he who turns dawn to darkness, and treads the high places of the earth—the Lord God Almighty is his name.

Amos 4:13

New Testament

In John Austin Baker's essay, "Biblical Views of Nature," we're told that "in contrast with the Hebrew Scriptures, the New Testament has relatively little to say about nature."[58] Although true, Jesus and the early Christians certainly refer to God's creation in speech and as a preference for the outdoors. Raymond C. Van Leeuwen summarizes the contrast in a different perspective, "The New Testament is a small book with an infinitely important but very limited agenda . . ."[59] centered on Jesus, the gospel, and the church. As you read these passages, notice how much of a role God plays in "sustaining" his creation.

The Birds of the Air

"Look at the birds of the air; they do not sow or reap or store away in barns, and yet your heavenly Father feeds them."

Matthew 6:26

God's Power

"He causes his sun to rise ... and sends rain ..."

Matthew 6:45

The Lilies of the Field

"And why do you worry about clothes? See how the lilies of the field grow."

Matthew 6:28

The Sparrow

"Are not two sparrows sold for a penny? Yet not one of them will fall to the ground apart from the will of your Father."

Matthew 10:29

Jesus' Praise

At that time, Jesus said, "I praise you, Father, Lord of heaven and earth . . ."

Matthew 11:25

Heaven, Earth, and Sea

"Sovereign Lord," they said, "you made the heaven and the earth and the sea, and everything in them."

Acts 4:24

Lord of Heaven and Earth

"The God who made the world and everything in it is the Lord of heaven and earth and does not live in temples built by hands."

Acts 17:24

Evidence of God's Power and Nature

For since the creation of the world God's invisible qualities—his eternal power and divine nature—have been clearly seen, being understood from what has been made . . .

Romans 1:20

God as Gardener

. . . only God . . . makes things grow.

1 Corinthians 3:7

The Earth and its Fullness

"The earth is the Lord's, and everything in it."

1 Corinthians 10:26

God Supplies

Now he who supplies seed to the sower and bread for food will also supply and increase your store of seed and will enlarge the harvest of your righteousness.

2 Corinthians 9:10

In the Beginning

"In the beginning, O Lord, you laid the foundations of the earth, and the heavens are the work of your hands."

Hebrews 1:10

Faith and Creation

By faith we understand that the universe was formed at God's command, so that what is seen was not made out of what was visible.

Hebrews 10:3

–6–

Reflections and Poems Praising God's Creation

Over the years, the grandeur and majesty of God's creation has moved many writers and poets to describe their observations in vivid words and language. These selections are primarily derived from individuals of the Judeo-Christian tradition and reflect a variety of secondary sources. When known, the author is given full credit. In addition, liberty was taken to title the untitled quotations for the reader's easy reference. On occasion, editing has eliminated phrases less relevant to the book's theme of creation praise and care. Finally, the quotations and poems have been alphabetized (by title).

A Forest Hymn

The groves were God's first temples.

William Cullen Bryant

A Million Miracles

O Son of God, perform a miracle for me: change my heart. You, whose crimson blood redeems mankind, whiten my heart.

It is you who makes the sun bright and the ice sparkle; you who makes the rivers flow and the salmon leap.

Your skilled hand makes the nut tree blossom, and the corn turn golden; your spirit composes the songs of the birds and the buzz of the bees.

Your creation is a million wondrous miracles, beautiful to behold. I ask of you just one more miracle: beautify my soul.

Anonymous Irish prayer

Ascending to God

In contemplation of created things,
By steps we may ascend to God.

John Milton

Be a Gardener

Be a gardener
Dig and ditch
Toil and sweat,
And turn the earth upside down
And seek the deepness
And water the plants in time.
Continue this work
And make sweet floods to run
And noble and abundant fruits
To spring.
Take this food and drink
And carry it to God
As your true worship.

Julian of Norwich

Break into Song

May none of God's wonderful works keep silence, night or morning.

Bright stars, high mountains, the depths of the seas, sources of rushing rivers:

May all these break into song as we sing to Father, Son, and Holy Spirit.

May all the angels in the heavens reply:

Amen! Amen! Amen!

Power, praise, honor eternal glory to God, the only Giver of grace.

Amen! Amen! Amen!

Anonymous (3rd century doxology)

Every Day

Let every day combine the beauty of spring, the brightness of summer, the abundance of autumn, and the repose of winter. And at the end of my life on earth, grant that I may come to see and to know you in the fullness of your glory. Amen.

Thomas Aquinas

God, Master-artist

Surely, everything that comes from the hand of such a Master-artist as God has something in it of himself!

C. H. Spurgeon

In the Woods

Almighty one, in the woods I am blessed.
Happy is everyone in the woods.
Every tree speaks of thee.
O God! What glory in the woodland!
On the heights in peace—peace to serve him.

Ludwig van Beethoven

Look Around You

In the name of God, stop a moment, close your work, look around you.

Leo Tolstoy

Moon and Stars

Lord Jesus Christ, you are the gentle moon and joyful stars that watch over the darkest night. You are the source of all peace reconciling the whole universe to the Father. You are the source of all rest, calming troubled hearts and bringing sleep to weary bodies. You are the sweetness that fills our minds with quiet joy and can turn the worst nightmares into dreams of heaven. May I dream of your sweetness, rest in your arms, be at one with your Father, and be comforted in the knowledge that you always watch over me.

Erasmus

Our Home

O God, we thank you for this earth, our home; for the wide sky and the blessed sun; for the salt sea and the running water; for the everlasting hills and the never resting winds; for the trees and the common grass underfoot.

We thank you for our senses by which we hear the songs of birds, and see the splendor of the summer fields and taste of the autumn fruits and rejoice in the feel of the snow and smell the breath of the spring.

Grant us a heart wide open to all this beauty; and save our souls from being so blind that we pass unseeing when even the common thornbush is aflame with your glory, O God our creator, who lives and reigns forever and ever. Amen.

Walter Rauschenbush

Protection

Protect me, My Lord; my boat is so small, and your ocean so big.

Breton fishermen's prayer

Shining Stars

The sun and the stars shining glorify God. They stand where he placed them, they move where he bid them. "The heavens declare the glory of God." They glorify God, but they do not know it. The birds sing to him, the thunder speaks of his terror, the lion is like his strength, the sea is like his greatness, the honey like his sweetness; they are something like him, they make him known, they tell of him, they give him glory, but they do not know they do.

Gerard Manley Hopkins

Take a Trip

As often as you can, take a trip out to the fields to pray.
All the grasses will join you.
They will enter your prayers and give you strength to sing praises to God.

Rabbi Nahman of Bratslav

Teach Us

Lord, thou sendest down rain upon the uncounted million of the forest, and givest the trees to drink exceedingly. We are here upon this isle a few handfuls of men, and how many myriads upon myriads of stalwart trees! Teach us the lesson of the trees. The sea around us, which this rain recruits, teems with the race of fish; teach us, Lord, the meaning of the fishes. Let us see ourselves for what we are, one out of the countless number of clans of thy handiwork. When we would despair, let us remember that these also please and serve Thee.

Robert Louis Stevenson

The Canticle of the Creatures

Most High, all-powerful, good Lord, yours are the praises, the glory, the honor, and all blessing. To you alone, Most High, do they belong, and no human is worthy to mention your name.

Praised be you, my Lord, with all your creatures, above all Brother Sun, who is the day and through whom you give us light. He is beautiful and radiant with great splendor; and bears a likeness of you, Most High One.

Praised be you, my Lord, through Sister Moon and the stars, in heaven you formed them clear and precious and beautiful.

Praised be you, my Lord, through Brother Wind, and through the air, cloudy and serene, and every kind of weather through which you cherish your creatures.

Praised be you, my Lord, through Sister Water, which is very useful and humble and precious and chaste.

Praised be you, my Lord, through Brother Fire, through whom you light the night, and he is beautiful and playful and robust and strong.

Praised be you, my Lord, through our Sister Mother Earth, who sustains and governs us, and who produces varied fruits with colored flowers and herbs.

Francis of Assisi

The Hazelnut

God showed me in my palm,
a little thing round as a ball,
about the size of a hazelnut.
I looked at it with the eye of understanding
and asked myself:
"What is this thing?"
And I was answered:
"It is everything that is."
I wondered how it survived
since it seemed so little,
as though it could disintegrate in a second
into nothingness.
The answer came:
"It exists and always will exist,
because God loves it."
Just so does everything have being
because of God's love.

Julian of Norwich

The Riches of God's Creation

Lord God, we praise you for those riches of your
creation which we shall never see:
for stars whose light will never reach the Earth;
for species of living things that were born,
that flourished and perished
before mankind appeared in the world;
for patterns and colors in the flowers,
which only insect eyes are able to see;
for strange, high music
that humans can never hear.
Lord God, you see everything that you have made and
behold it is very good.

Anonymous

Thy Sun

We thank thee, Lord, for the glory of the late days and the excellent face of thy sun . . . We thank thee for good news received. We thank thee for the pleasures we have enjoyed and for those we have been able to confer. And now, when the clouds gather and rain impends over the forest and our house, permit us not to be cast down; let us not lose the savor of past mercies and past pleasures; but, like the voice of a bird singing in the rain, let grateful memory survive in the hour of darkness.

Robert Louis Stevenson

James Woodrow

Thy Whole Creation

But let my soul praise Thee that it may love Thee,
And let it tell Thee Thy mercies that it may praise Thee.
Without ceasing Thy whole creation speaks Thy praise—
The spirit of every man by the words that his mouth directs to Thee,
Animals and lifeless matter by the mouth of those who look upon them.
That so our soul rises out of its mortal weariness unto Thee,
Helped upward by the things Thou has made
And passing beyond them unto Thee who has wonderfully made them:
And there refreshment is and strength unfailing. Amen.

Augustine

Treasure in Nature

If we are children of God, we have a tremendous treasure in nature and will realize that it is holy and sacred. We will see God reaching out to us in every wind that blows, every sunrise and sunset, every cloud in the sky, every flower that blooms, and every leaf that fades, if we will only begin to use our blinded thinking to visualize it.

Oswald Chambers

We Thank Thee

For this new morning with its light . . .

For flowers that bloom about our feet,
For tender grass, so fresh, so sweet,
For song of bird and hum of bee,
For all things fair we hear or see,

Father in Heaven, we thank Thee.

For blue of stream and blue of sky,
For pleasant shade of branches high,
For fragrant air and cooling breeze,
For beauty of the blooming trees,

Father we thank Thee.

Ralph Waldo Emerson

You Are the Sun

Lord Jesus Christ, you are the sun that always rises, but never sets. You are the source of all life, creating and sustaining every living thing.

Erasmus

DEVELOPING A PERSONAL APPROACH WITH GOD

–7–

Experiencing God's Creation

"Immediately, when we see or experience any
natural phenomenon, when we see a flower, a
butterfly, a tree, when we feel the evening breeze
flow over us or wade in a stream of clear water,
our natural response is immediate, intuitive,
transforming, ecstatic. Everywhere we find
ourselves invaded by the world of the sacred."

Thomas Berry, *When the Trees Say Nothing*[60]

Overview

This section was especially designed with a workbook
format in mind, providing practical, hands-on insights into
how we can praise God as creator and sustainer of his
magnificent garden we call Earth as well as how we can
use nature to personally connect with God. We do this
by appreciating our inter-connectedness with this world
and by accepting ownership as caretakers for his precious,
fragile garden. We do this by daily celebrating the joy of
creation.

On a recent vacation in Tennessee's Great Smoky Mountains and at the end of a beautiful tree-shaded trail, I found myself with a score of others who had also hiked to the base of Abrams Falls. Everyone was taking pictures, chatting, snacking, swimming, and sitting on rocks while admiring nature's beauty—I'm sure many praising God in their own way as well. Yet, none that I could see had sat down quietly with a Bible or other literature, so I found myself again appreciating the need and value of a devotional book that would serve as an easy-to-carry, outdoor companion for celebrating God's creation in our daily walk with God.

Life's hectic schedule requires us to set aside time to simply rest, and for many of us, there is no better place to relax and reenergize ourselves than outdoors and in the quietness and serenity of nature. And while we may continue to enjoy many of our devotionals indoors, we can quickly remind ourselves of the power of reinvigoration that comes as a result of our outdoor experiences, as well as how we were drawn closer to God. Many of us also find nature to be a good place to work out problems—and to seek "balance" in our lives—as well as to praise God.

The result of our presence in God's creation is an opportunity to praise him, but it's also one of renewal, of strength of purpose (that God has a plan for us just as the lilies of the field).

Self-Assessment

Are you a naturalist? Although all readers can benefit by this book, this informal inventory was created to help you determine the strength of your "naturalist" tendencies. Simply respond to each of the statements using a 10-point scale (1 = no interest, 2-4 = low interest, 5 = moderate interest, 6-9 = high interest, 10 = highest interest). The inventory is not an exam. There are no right or wrong answers. Your score, though, will assist you toward better understanding your naturalist temperament.

____ 1. Many of my most cherished childhood memories are of activities, play, and vacation time in the outdoors.

____ 2. Listening to a CD titled, *The Sounds of Nature,* is appealing to me.

____ 3. Watching nature, travel, and other TV channels that transport me into nature and the outdoors is attractive to me.

____ 4. Receiving a gift book of photographs called, *The Best of Nature,* is something I would enjoy.

_____ 5. When I plan a vacation, I frequently consider whether it will allow me to spend lots of time in the out-of-doors.

_____ 6. I would rather exercise outside than inside.

_____ 7. I wish more opportunities were available for my congregation to collectively worship outdoors.

_____ 8. When I'm surrounded by nature—the meadows, woods, or water—I feel close to God.

_____ 9. When I need to escape the worry and stress of life, I seek to go outdoors.

_____10. Many of my favorite hymns and scriptures relate to God's creation.

Total score = _____

The highest possible score is 100 points, and the higher the score, the stronger your predisposition as a "naturalist." If your total score is 50 or higher, this book is likely to serve your naturalist tendencies well as you celebrate God's creation in the outdoors.

Journal and Worksheets

For the reader who also likes to write, journaling can be a very rewarding process. Writing about our observations and memories of outdoor experiences can serve as a valuable tool for creating our own set of devotional exercises for celebrating God's creation. One of my first journaling efforts follows, which also seemed appropriate to bear this book's title: "Under sun and moon, all nature sings, Creator of this magnificent earth. You and only you are worthy of praise."

A variety of journaling techniques can help us record our special moments in nature. Some examples follow, with space for note-taking:

James Woodrow

List ways and times when you use your senses to appreciate God's creation, his garden.

Sights:

Sounds:

Smells:

Tastes:

Touch:

Write about your childhood memories in the outdoors. Reflect on them.

Create some personal prayers from your experiences with nature, ultimately thanking and praising God.

James Woodrow

Create a series of questions for your outdoor reflections on the Creator's creation.

Ask yourself what was it like when you talked to an animal, maybe a bird in the backyard or a squirrel in the woods, and thanked God for that special connection with his creation?

Consider how you can learn to be still, and listen to the sounds (and silence) of God's creation.

Write about your appreciation for the smallest of God's creation—for example, fallen leaves, grains of sand, ugly bugs, blades of grass, and colorful butterflies.

Write down what comes to mind when you think back on each of the seasons and your outdoor experiences with them, knowing how God loves each stage of his creation.

Spring:

Summer:

Autumn:

Winter:

Although each creature has meaning and usefulness in this world, write about your favorite creatures and why they're special in your eyes.

Build phrases about the "special places" where you find it especially meaningful to spend time communing with God and celebrating his creation.

James Woodrow

When sitting at one your favorite places in the out-of-doors, describe what wonders of God's creation you see when you:

Look up

Look out (or across)

Look down

What makes your favorite hymns, scriptures, and quotations special to you?

How would you describe the "mystery" of God's creation?

Special Places and Personal Reflections

In addition, several pages have been set aside to enter personal drawings or descriptions of your "Special Places" where you feel a unique connection with God as creator. There's also a "Personal Reflections" section at the bottom of each page for your personal prayers and devotions. These techniques will serve you well in your search to clarify and define personal ways of celebrating God's creation through thanksgiving, meditation, pray, song, and praise.

Special Places

Personal Reflections

Special Places

Personal Reflections

James Woodrow

Special Places

Personal Reflections

Special Places

Personal Reflections

Special Places

Personal Reflections

Special Places

Personal Reflections

Special Places

Personal Reflections

Special Places

Personal Reflections

Special Places

Personal Reflections

Special Places

Personal Reflections

Websites

Numerous churches and faith-based organizations now provide an array of resources for individuals, groups, and congregations interested in creation care. The author does not promote or advocate any of these organizations, but offers a sample of websites with the purpose of providing additional perspectives and information about this growing environmental movement among Christians.

Named after the Portuguese word for "the rock," **A Rocha** (http://www.arocha.org) is "a Christian nature conservation organization which, inspired by God's love, engages in scientific research, environmental education, and community-based conservation projects."

The board chair of **Au Sable Institute** (http://ausable.org) states: "We are a Christian institute of environmental studies with the mission of bringing both the Christian community and the public at large to a fuller, deeper, and better understanding of the stewardship of God's creation."

Blessed Earth (http://blessedearth.org) is a "biblically based educational nonprofit that inspires and equips Christians to become better stewards of the earth. Through outreach to churches, campuses, and other organizations, we build bridges that promote measurable environmental change and meaningful spiritual growth."

Serving the UK, Kenya, and the USA, **Care of Creation** (http://www.careofcreation.net) was established "to bring together two important themes: love for God's people and love for God's world."

The **Center for Environmental Leadership** (http://www. center4eleadership.org) is "devoted to two things: helping individuals, institutions, and communities act on their convictions to care for creation and educating the next generation of Christian environmental leaders."

Christ United Methodist Church (http://www. christgreensboro.org) provides a creation care series of sermons, tips, and additional resources.

The website for the **Church of the Brethren** contains a variety of resources on creation care (http://www.brethren. org) with an introduction that "God's good creation is a vital part of the peace and justice we are seeking. A right relationship with God calls for a harmonious relationship with all of creation."

Designed for evangelical leaders and environmental scientists, **Creation Care for Pastors** (http://www. creationcareforpastors.com) is designed to "serve pastors who are interested in a growing emphasis within the Christian community."

As a study abroad program for Christian college students, the **Creation Care Study Program** (http://creationcsp.org) offers academic semesters for college credit in Belize and New Zealand.

Eden Vigil (http://www.edenvigil.org) is an "environmental missions initiative whose purpose is: to love Christ and His created through mobilizing and serving those who combine church-planting and creation care among least-reached peoples."

The **Evangelical Environmental Network** (http://creationcare.org) is "a ministry that seeks to educate, equip, inspire, and mobilize Christians in their effort to care for God's creation, to be faithful stewards of God's provision, and to advocate for actions and policies that honor God and protect the environment."

Lutherans Restoring Creation (http://www.lutheransrestoringcreation.org) is "a grassroots movement within the ELCA, seeking to foster care for God's good creation in all expressions of our church's life. [It] is a program designed to encourage the Evangelical Lutheran Church in America (ELCA) to incorporate care for creation into its full life and mission at all levels."

Focusing on Mennonite congregations, the **Mennonite Creation Care Network** (http://mennocreationcare.org) is "a faith-based network of people engaged in caring for creation."

Student oriented, **Renewal** (http://renewingcreation.org) is "a Christ-centered creation care network that focuses on living in right relationship with God."

These resources are designed to form a starting point toward developing a more informed understanding of creation care.

Index of Devotional Resources

H

I

J

K

L

Notes

1: Introduction

1. Paul Hoversten, "Flight Through Heavens Awes Glenn," *USA Today* (November 2, 1998).
2. F. Lynne Bachleda, *Canticles of the Earth* (Chicago, Loyola Press, 2004), x.
3. Article Two, *Belgic Confession* (Christian Reformed Church, 1618).
4. Steven Bouma-Prediger, *For the Beauty of the Earth: A Christian Vision for Creation Care* (Grand Rapids, Baker Academic, 2001), 14.
5. Tom Price, "What Vision Will Preserve Anabaptist Identity in the 21st Century?' Scholars Ask," *Gospel Herald* (October 1994), 10.

2: A Philosophy of Stewardship

1. Steven Bouma-Prediger, *For the Beauty of the Earth: A Christian Vision for Creation Care* (Grand Rapids, Baker Academic, 2001), 70.
2. Robert Booth Fowler, cited in *The Greening of Protestant Thought* (Chapel Hill, University of North Carolina, 1995), 47.
3. Larry Penner, cited in "Conference Aims to Create Green Theology." *Mennonite* 110 (March 14, 1995), 13-14.

4. Bouma-Prediger, *For the Beauty of the Earth,* 118.

5. Newt Gingrich & Terry L. Maple, cited in *A Contract with the Earth* (Baltimore, The Johns Hopkins University Press, 2007), 185.

6. Scott Hoezee, *Remember Creation: God's World of Wonder and Delight* (Grand Rapids, Eerdmans, 1998), 45.

7. Joseph Sittler, "Evangelism and the Care of the Earth." In *Preaching and the Witnessing Community,* edited by Herman Stuemplfle (Philadelphia, Fortress, 1973), 102.

8. Bouma-Prediger, *For the Beauty of the Earth,* 154-179.

9. David Kline, "God's Spirit and a Theology for Living." In *Creation & the Environment: An Anabaptist Perspective on a Sustainable World,* edited by Calvin Redekop (Baltimore, The Johns Hopkins University Press, 2000), 61.

10. Ibid, 63.

11. Ibid, 63.

12. C.W. Lowdermilk, *Conquest of the Land through Seven Thousand Years.* Bulletin 99 (Washington, U.S. Department of Agriculture, 1948), 30.

13. Kline, "God's Spirit and a Theology for Living," 69.

14. Laurel Kearns, "Saving the Creation: Christian Environmentalism in the United States," *Sociology of Religion* 57 (Spring 1996), 58.

15. David Orr, *Ecological Literacy: Education and the Transition to a Postmodern World* (Albany, State University of New York, 1992), 92.

16. Bouma-Prediger, *For the Beauty of the Earth,* 22.

17. Ibid, 22-23.

18. Gingrich & Maple, *A Contract with the Earth,* 197.

19. Ibid, 3.

20. Delores Histand Friesen, *Living More with Less: Study/Action Guide* (Scottdale, PA, Herald Press, 1981), 99.

21. Levi Miller, *Our People: The Amish and Mennonites of Ohio* (Scottdale, PA, Herald Press, 1983), 6.

22. Janet Willard, "Amish Farm by Rules of Church and God." In *The Amish: A Culture, a Religion, a Way of Life.* Special section of Holmes County Hub (June 1992), 25.

23. Calvin Redekop, "The Environmental Challenge before Us." In *Creation & the Environment: An Anabaptist Perspective on a Sustainable World,* edited by Calvin Redekop (Baltimore, The Johns Hopkins University Press, 2000), 213, and *Mennonite Central Committee Statement on the Environment,* Item No. 29 (September 1994).

24. Bouma-Prediger, *For the Beauty of the Earth,* 135.

25. Ibid, 187.

3: Practices for Communing with God

1. Fyodor Dostoevsky, *The Brothers Karamazov* (Chicago: Encyclopedia Britannica, Great Books, 1952), 167.

2. Margaret Ruth Miles, cited in *The Travail of Nature,* by H. Paul Santmire (Philadelphia, Fortress, 1985), 90.

3. Roger D. Sorrell, *St. Francis of Assisi and Nature* (New York: Oxford University Press, 1988), 29.

4. Martin Buber, *Tales of the Hasidim: Early Masters* (New York: Schocken Books, Inc., 1948), 111.

5. Gary Thomas, *Sacred Pathways: Discover Your Soul's Path to God* (Grand Rapids, Zondervan Publishing House, 1996), 50.

6. Richard J. Foster, *Celebration of Discipline: The Path to Spiritual Growth* (San Francisco, Harper & Row, 1978), 63.

7. The author wants to give credit to Steven Bouma-Prediger in his powerful book, *For the Beauty of the Earth,* for many of these ideas and metaphors.

8. Susan Power Bratton, *Christianity, Wilderness and Wildlife* (Scranton: University of Scranton Press, 1993), 90-91.

9. Thomas, *Sacred Pathways*, 44.

10. Ibid, 50.

11. Sermons on the Gospel of John, cited in Santmire, *The Travail of Nature,* 131.

12. Thomas, *Sacred Pathways*, 50.

13. Bonaventure, cited in Santmire, *The Travail of Nature,* 99.

14. Thomas, *Sacred Pathways*, 45.

15. Ibid, 46.

16. Gingrich & Maple, *A Contract with the Earth,* 180.

17. Foster, *Celebration of Discipline,* 80-81.

18. Bouma-Prediger, *For the Beauty of the Earth,* 145.

19. Ibid, 146.

20. Ibid, 166.

21. Henry David Thoreau, *Walden and Other Writings,* edited by Joseph Wood Kruthch (New York, Bantam, 1981), 115.

22. Bouma-Prediger, *For the Beauty of the Earth,* 167-168.

4: Hymns and Songs

1. Lawrence Hart, "The Earth Is a Song Made Visible." In *Creation & the Environment: An Anabaptist Perspective on a Sustainable World,* edited by Calvin Redekop (Baltimore, The Johns Hopkins University Press, 2000), 179.

2. Alton H. Howard, compiler and editor, *Songs of Faith and Praise,* Shape Note Edition (West Monroe, LA, Howard Publishing Co., 1994).

5: Holy Scriptures

1. Steven Bouma-Prediger, *For the Beauty of the Earth: A Christian Vision for Creation Care* (Grand Rapids, Baker Academic, 2001), 15.

2. Wendell Berry, *Sex, Economy, Freedom, and Community.* In *Canticles of the Earth,* edited by F. Lynne Bachleda (Chicago, Loyola Press, 2004), 171.

3. International Bible Society, *The Holy Bible, New International Version,* (Grand Rapids, The Zondervan Corporation, 1973, 1978, 1984).

4. John Austin Baker, "Biblical Views of Nature." In *Liberating Life: Contemporary Approaches to Ecological Theology,* edited by Charles Birch, William Eakin, & Jay B. McDaniel (Maryknoll, NY, Orbis Books, 1990), 20.

5. Raymond C. Van Leeuwen, "Christ's Resurrection and the Creation's Vindication." In *The Environment and the Christian: What Does the New Testament Say about the Environmnent?,* edited by Calvin B. Dewitt (Grand Rapids, Baker Book House, 1991), 60.

7: Experiencing God's Creation

1. Thomas Berry, "Foreword." In *When the Trees Say Nothing: Writings on Nature/Thomas Merton,* edited by Kathleen Deignan (Notre Dame, IN, Sorin Books, 2003).